BEHIND THE
CAPE

THE ULTIMATE COMIC BOOK HERO EXPLAINED

D0099395

ROB JEFFERSON

ISBN 978-1-63353-390-5

"Krypton bred me, but it was Earth that gave me all I am."

Man of Steel, Vol. 1 #6 December, 1986

Dedication:

To the friends, family and fans, without whom
I would have never made it this far.

TABLE OF CONTENTS

Foreword

Probably one of the most asked questions I hear comic book and comic book movies fans ask each other is: what was your first comic? It means a lot in the world of comics, because it is what set people off on the path of they are on now. Did you start with the ultra-heroic superhero, the one who's never willing to kill and friends with the world? Or was your first superhero a brooding antihero that everyone hated to be around? It's what helped steer you down the path of the comics you loved. You either came out of that first comic book loving this style of superhero and sought out many more like them, or followed their friends through their comics. Or adversely, you came out of reading that hero hating what they stood for and steered in the opposite direction.

My first hero was Superman. When I was a young child, my father brought home the comic Superman Time and Time Again. I barely even remember it at this point in my life, but I remember Superman fought dinosaurs and was traveling through time. I honestly don't even know if the dinosaur scene was in there or if that's my mind making the scene up. But whatever I read in that original comic steered me towards Superman: a hero that is an alien to our world, yet instead of becoming a villain was raised with a proper upbringing. He showed that you can become a product of your environment. He represented truth and justice, and he fought for what was morally right. He was the leader of the Justice League, more often than not, and what other superheroes looked up to. For me, this was what a superhero should be.

The world has seemingly agreed because of the popularity of Superman. While I have seen it disputed in some locations, there is a valid argument that the Superman symbol is the most recognizable symbol in the world, even more recognizable than the Christian cross due to there being varying religions around the world. This says something about what the symbol of Superman means. You don't see it on gangs or in the middle of a riot. You see it when people want to be heroes. The imagery of Clark Kent opening his button-up shirt and running in as Superman is seen as a heroic act.

I think we'll never see another superhero revered on the scale that Superman is. He is one of the few superheroes that everyone has their own version of in their heads. Some want a more conflicted version, some want a version who is always right. Some view him as a godlike hero, while some view him as an alien stuck on our planet and forced to adopt earth as his home. But in the end, regardless of which version you prefer, everyone knows he is supposed to be the hero: the one that stands up for the little guys and protects them.

Superman is where the archetype of the Superhero started, and there is a reason for that.

Benny Potter, creator of the Comicstorian and author of The Rise of Comic Book Movies

CHAPTER

1

The Dawn of Superman

During the last weekend of January 2016, I was invited to PAX South in San Antonio Texas, a newly launched branch of the larger Penny Arcade Exposition known as PAX Prime, a yearly celebration of gaming culture bringing both developers and fans together in an effort to advertise and showcase new games by both established and independent companies. During my time in San Antonio, a friend of mine and I were to host a panel dedicated to comic books in film and the nature of comic book reboots. I've long since felt that when speaking directly to an audience about a topic they may be unfamiliar with, the best course of action is to ask questions in order to provide a better understanding of the source material. Taking this route, I asked how many people were unsure of where to start in comic books, found them to be confusing, or simply had a passing interest in them.

Assuming that I'm recalling this accurately, I would say somewhere around 80 percent or better were unsure of where to start and did find comic books to be confusing, but they also had a desire to learn more. Having already been in the process of working on this book, I put this information to use in an effort to both provide you with a history of print media in the United States, as well as how the introduction of Comic Books came in the form of a gradual evolution.

For many people, the recent explosions of Marvel and DC based films and television shows have shaped a desire to understand why comic book creations like Spider-Man, Batman and others are so popular, as well as how the entire comic book industry came into existence. While the contents of the book will answer those questions and more, it's important to note that much of what came before the creation of comic books was rooted in pulp magazines and newspaper strips.

During most of the United States' early history from the establishment of the original Colonies up to the late 1700's, print media was largely isolated to Newspapers which ranged anywhere from The New England Courant focusing on shipping reports, letters to the editor and gossip from neighboring towns, to the Massachusetts Spy and Patriotic Press, both of which maintained rhetoric that was used as a tactic for fostering cohesiveness among the Pre-Revolutionary War colonies without advocating open rebellion against the rule of England under King George III.

Furthermore, following the 1804 expedition of Lewis and Clark along with the subsequent western expansion, Newspapers grew in number, becoming as diverse as the towns on the western frontier meaning that by 1835, there were hundreds of newspapers in circulation including the Sandusky Register in Ohio, the Picayune in Louisiana, the Post and Courier in Pennsylvania and the Augusta Chronicle in Georgia. While most of these publications were poorly by written by today's standards due to a lack of access to the fledgling public education system which didn't begin to become compulsory until the 1850's, the purpose of these varying newspapers was served in that elected officials often wrote articles in the papers of their home cities keeping people abreast of political developments, trade and so on. As a result, the newspaper system became a kind of rallying point for bringing together an otherwise fragmented series of territories allowing society to become wholly aware of what was happening throughout their nation and especially at its center regarding the Governmental body.

Where there is no definitive point at which newspaper comic strips originated owing in large part to the idea that regional newspapers were developing their own comic strips as a way to provide diversity and access potential customers who were not interested in news involving politics and trade, on the whole, the most famous of these original strips came in 1895 with The Yellow Kid. Written and drawn by Richard M. Outcault and published in Joseph Pulitzer's New York World, a New York based newspaper, which ran between 1860 and 1931, the stories of The Yellow Kid focused on Mickey Dugan, a bald, snaggle-toothed barefoot boy who wore an oversized yellow nightshirt.

> ...regional newspapers were developing their own comic strips as a way to provide diversity and access potential customers who were not interested in news involving politics and trade...

Designed to be a reflection of Outcault's experience with poor boys in society who were often seen in New York's tenement ghetto's, the popularity of The Yellow Kid was found in his goofy grin as well as ragged and peculiar slang. While these stories ran alongside several others within New York World as part of a comic series titled Hogan's Alley, the concept gave way to a rivalry between Pulitzer's New York World and William Randolph Hearst's

New York Journal-American creating an explosion of newspaper comic strips with the two competing companies acquiring regional works including Randolph Dirk's 1897 strip The Katzenjammer Kids which established concepts like speech balloons, and Jimmy Swinnerton's 1892 strip The Little Bears which provided the first recurring characters in a comic series.

During this time, Frank Munsey, a resident of New York City was publishing a magazine titled The Golden Argosy, and where the stories contained within targeted children as its main demographic, because the reader base began to lose interest as they grew into teenagers or else were not able to access the money necessary to maintain their subscription to the magazine, the Golden Argosy ultimately failed and nearly led Munsey into bankruptcy. However, after recognizing the popularity of the comic strips found in Pulitzer and Hearst's newspaper companies which targeted adults, Munsey shifted his focus from Children's stories to Pulp Fiction, a style of storytelling focusing on lurid and run-of-the-mill low quality subject matter. With few publishers in this market at the time, Munsey's work flourished and went from several thousand copies per month to over five hundred thousand.

Largely considered to be the foundation for which the notion of Pulp Magazine's originated, in 1903, a company called Street & Smith formed in 1855 by Francis Scott Street and Francis Shubel Smith began to dip their toes in the market of Pulp magazines with their launch of The Popular Magazine, which featured short stories, novellas and full novels. Where The Popular Magazine went on to become the first Pulp Magazine to produce full covers, much like the competition between Joseph Pulitzer and William Randolph Hearst, the competition between the Golden Argosy and The Popular Magazine ushered in a series of other competitors who looked to cash in on the emerging market meaning that between the late-1890's going into the early 1930's, pulp magazines grew to not only include adult oriented material, but also heroic themes in the form of The Shadow, Doc Savage and The Phantom Detective, all of whom would come together and form Superman as he was created by Jerry Siegel and Joe Shuster.

...pulp magazines grew to not only include adult oriented material, but also heroic themes in the form of The Shadow, Doc Savage and The Phantom Detective, all of whom would come together and form Superman as he was created by Jerry Siegel and Joe Shuster.

That said, while the Superman we know today with the red cape and blue uniform did not appear until Action Comics issue number one in 1938, the origins of Superman can be traced back to his creation at the hands of

Joe Schuster in 1933. During this same year, Schuster would introduce his creation to a fellow student at Glenville High school in Cleveland Ohio named Jerry Siegel who would go on to publish Superman in his own series titled Science Fiction: The Advance Guard of Future Civilization.

Focusing on fictional stories, which included King Kong, issue number 3 titled Reign of The Superman introduced the Man of Steel as a telepathic villain bent on World Domination. In a 1981 interview by BBC titled Superman: The Comic Strip Hero, Siegel and Shuster had stated that in 1934 following Shuster's creation of Superman, Siegel had revamped the character, going through a series of drafts, and as the two worked together, these changes grew to include the inclusion of the now famous boots, belt and cape, the later of which was designed to give the illusion of movement as Superman flew threw the air. Moreover, in the eyes of Siegel & Schuster, the 1930's were a time of social unrest and economic turmoil for the United States.

It had been four years since the onset of the Great Depression and although things were taking a turn for the better, for many people the effects were still being felt. Suicides, robberies, homeless and a general sense of scarcity were all still a part of American Life and with the possibility of a second World War looming in the background, society needed someone to look up to; something to inspire them with hope, even if only for a short time.

...Siegel and Schuster modeled this newest version of Superman after three important characters that represented the strength and resiliency of the human spirit...

To this end, in addition to the various heroes found within Pulp magazines, Siegel and

Schuster modeled this newest version of Superman after three important characters that represented the strength and resiliency of the human Spirit. The first was Hugo Danner of the famed novel Gladiator written by Phillip Wiley in 1930. The result of an experiment by his father, Hugo Danner was born with incredible strength, but was told to keep his powers hidden due to the fact that societies' inability to understand him would make him a target of fear and ignorance. The second was Hercules; the Roman name used for Heracles, the famed son of Zeus and Alcmene who imbued the very essence of courage, strength and ingenuity. Finally the third inspiration for Superman came from Sampson, a man of Biblical origin who received incredible strength from God.

Following this, and with their newest creation in hand, Jerry Siegel and Joe Schuster spent the next six years trying to find a publisher who would take Superman and bring him to the mainstream. It was during this time that Superman was introduced to Consolidated Book Publishers, a distributor based out of Chicago Illinois providing various bookstores with sellable content in the hopes that the company would include Superman in their various hero related materials which included a series called Detective Dan: Secret Operative No. 48. However, Consolidated Publishing had only distributed one story of Detective Dan and had no intention of moving forward with further distribution due to a lack of sales, and so while they sent and encouraging letter to Siegel and Schuster praising their work, with multiple publishers or distributors including Educational Comics and United Feature Syndicate all rejecting their idea, Schuster became fed up, leading him to destroy all of the pages of Superman with the exception of the cover, which was saved from the fire by Jerry Siegel. However, as Siegel and Schuster recovered from their disappointment and continued their efforts to find someone to print the story of Superman, another comic book icon was emerging: a Tennessee native and writer with a penchant for creating short stories, who would go on to develop what many consider to be the very first Comic Book.

CHAPTER

2

Action Comics

A former member of the United States Calvary, in 1934 Malcolm Wheeler Nicholson launched National Allied Publications in an effort to capitalize on the success of newspaper strips and Pulp magazines by combining them into a wholly new printing format. However, Nicholson soon found that companies like Dell Publications, a New York City based publishing company which owned and distributed the Famous Funnies comic strip was unwilling to take a risk on his newly established company due to fear that his work wouldn't sell. Refusing to be left out of the fledgling market, Nicholson made history for the first time in launching his own comic book in the form of New Fun Comics number one.

Deviating away from the re-printed material in Dell Publications' Famous Funnies, New Fun Comics contained a series of comedic stories involving characters designed by Nicholson himself. However, because the company was new and money was slow, Nicholson made history a second time when he became the first comic book company to offer advertising space in his works to offset the costs of production. While Malcolm Wheeler Nicholson would go on to use these funds as a way to launch a second publication titled Adventure Comics, he also discovered that because Famous Funnies was selling so well as it contained characters that the general public was already familiar with, distributors were hesitant to invest in this content because it had never been tested before. In their eyes, Famous Funnies had an established market and Dell publications alongside other publishers had all proven themselves capable of producing content that customers would buy. As a result, and with money running out fast as well as virtually all doors being closed in his face, Nicholson found himself in a partnership with a man named Harry Donnefeld.

As the Owner and operator of Independent News, while Harry Donnefeld had occasionally experimented with magazine markets, his involvement in Pulp titles like Spicy Adventures and Spicy Detective drew the attention of Nicholson who looked to use Independent News as a way to ensure the existence of New Fun Comics and Adventure Comics, as well as introduce a new publication in the form of Detective Comics. However, the decision came at a great cost in that assistance from Donenfeld required Malcom Wheeler Nicholson to sacrifice a large majority of the rights of his work in order to allow Harry Donenfeld to provide distribution.

Following this, with Nicholson and Donenfeld working together and forming a joint company called Detective Comics Incorporated under the Umbrella of National Allied Publications, the two began to hire various artist and writers to produce new ideas, and among those hired onto the Detective Comics branch were Siegel and Schuster. Where their early work in Detective Comics consisted of stories like Slam Bradley, a private detective with brawn, who with all intents and purposes is the spiritual predecessor to Batman, Siegel and Schuster also saw this as an opportunity to attempt to re-introduce Superman.

Unfortunately, because of the rapid growth of Detective Comics Incorporated and with the company receiving numerous concepts that were written or drawn by other aspiring creators, Siegel and Schuster's Superman was quite literally thrown into a pile and completely ignored. While the two continued their work on

Slam Bradley among other creations, Malcolm Wheeler Nicholson's decision to engage in business with Harry Donenfeld would come back to haunt him. Considered to be something of myth and hearsay, in the summer of 1938, Donenfeld sent Nicholson on a vacation for the purpose of brainstorming and creating new ideas for the company. During Nicholson's vacation however, Harry Donenfeld filed a lawsuit against Nicholson for failure to pay printing fees, and because Nicholson's vacation made it impossible for him to appear in Court, Donenfeld won the lawsuit by default judgment. As a result, Malcolm Wheeler Nicholson was forced out of Detective Comics Incorporated, and Harry Donenfeld obtained all rights to National Allied Publications and its properties, including Detective Comics Incorporated, which included all of the work produced by Nicholson himself.

With Nicholson out of the picture and Donenfeld in control of Detective Comics Incorporated, while he continued publication and distribution of New Fun Comics, Adventure Comics and Detective Comics he also sought to expand the existing line up of hero based content. Launching a fourth series in the form of Action Comics but short on material necessary to meet the printing deadline date, Donenfeld instructed Action Comics editor Vin Sullivan to find content that could quickly be added to issue number one. Sorting through a stack of write-ins, Vin Sullivan stumbled upon Superman and as a result, not only was he added to the roster of stories, he was placed on the cover.

> ...Vin Sullivan stumbled upon Superman and as a result, not only was he added to the roster of stories, he was placed on the cover.

Originally depicted as a child sent away on a dying world by an unknown scientist, the newborn was discovered by two passing motorists who took him to a local orphanage. While there, he demonstrated incredible strength and as the years passed, he was able to leap one-eighth of a mile, raise tremendous weights and run faster than an express train, all due to his advanced physiology and the fact this his race was endowed with incredible strength once they reached maturity. With the name Clark Kent acting as a disguise, Superman served to fight on the behalf of the common man battling criminals and Governmental corruption.

Within the pages of Action Comics number one, Siegel and Schuster also introduced Superman's main love interest in the form of Lois Lane, a tough as nails journalist whose name is actually a derivative of Lola Lane, one of three sisters who performed in a 1930's singing act. Considered by many to be the first lady of comics and the quintessential damsel in distress, in truth the development of her character was influenced by three individuals. Physically, Lois Lane was designed to look like Jo Ann Carter, the future wife of Jerry Siegel who had started her modeling career after posing for a series of drawings by Siegel while he was working on a concept for Lois Lane. In terms of personality, Siegel and Schuster drew inspiration from Torchy Blane, a no-nonsense reporter who did what it took to get the story and was played by Glenda Farrell in a series of 1930's films, as well as Elizabeth Cochran Seaman, an American Journalist, writer, industrialist, inventor and charity worker best known for having travelled around the world in seventy-two days.

For Siegel and Schuster, Lois Lane existing as a reporter and love interest for Superman was a combination that inspired elation, suspense and comedy among fans in that while working directly with Clark Kent, the banter between the two was a hallmark of their friendship, but as the love interest of Superman, in addition to grounding his character and making him more human despite his alien origins, fans always wondered if she would ever learn that Clark Kent and Superman were one and the same. However, following the release of Action Comics number one, Harry Donenfeld considered both the character of Superman and the concept to be ridiculous, and while he had intended to have Superman removed from publication and effectively locked away, his mind was changed when, as the legend goes, he approached a young boy at a comic book stand and when Donenfeld asked the boy why he was buying the comic the boy replied, "Because it's the one that has Superman."

> ...when Donenfeld asked the boy why he was buying the comic the boy replied, "Because it's the one that has Superman."

With sales of Action comics cementing that Superman was here to stay, the Golden age of Comics had begun, and the comic book industry was off to the races. Selling the rights to their creation for 130 dollars and a contract to provide material, the success of Superman saw Siegel and Schuster collaborating on the introduction of a solo series titled "Superman #1" which ran alongside Action Comics but differed in that the stories in the solo-series focused largely on Superman himself instead of frequently recurring characters like Lois Lane who normally appeared in Action Comics. During this time, the Man of Steel received his own radio show program titled: "The Adventures of Superman", and by 1941, the world was met with Superman's first Animated Film, created by Fleischer Studios, the now defunct animation studio based out of New York City. Not all was perfect for DC's newest creation however. While Superman's success saw the introduction of Batman who quickly became the standout star of Detective Comics and a rival that would remain one of Superman's closest competitors in both sales and popularity, the Golden age of Comics also saw an influx of characters similar to Superman, the closest of which was a hero named Captain Marvel. The 1939 brainchild of writer Bill Parker and artist CC Beck, Captain Marvel's popularity rivaled Superman's in that while the Man of Steel was the first Superhero, Captain Marvel had something that Superman did not have: a child with Superpowers.

> **...the lure of Superman came in the form of imagination and the possibility that his readers could live vicariously through his comics...**

With Comic Books becoming increasingly popular among young boys, the lure of Superman came in the form of imagination and the possibility that his readers could live vicariously through his comics and right the wrongs in their own lives using the Man of Steels fantastic powers. Capitalizing on this sentiment, Fawcett Comics, a division of Fawcett Publications looking to cash in on the rise of Superhero comics, introduced Captain Marvel as a young homeless boy named Billy Batson who was led to a Wizard named Shazam. Recognizing the financial struggles of Billy as well as the courage he displayed in the face of such hardship, the wizard bestowed upon Billy the power to become a Superhero by shouting the world Shazam. Since Captain Marvel provided fans with the belief that a child could become equal to Superman in virtually all forms, the sales of Captain Marvel soared and even led to a radio show that predated Superman's. Recognizing the success of Captain Marvel and that his character appeared to be a carbon copy of Superman, in 1941 DC filed a lawsuit on the grounds of Copyright Infringement, a case that would go on to remain in court for over 10 years.

By the time the 1940's came around, Superman was a mainstay in pop-culture, and at the time, the series consisted of one or two issue battles between himself and a gangster or villain. In the minds of Siegel and Schuster, in order for their creation to have longevity outside of this initial comic boom, Superman needed an arch villain who returned constantly to face him. However because Superman's abilities were largely physical, his nemesis needed to be the other half of the equation and possess a level of intelligence that would test the Man of Steel and push him to both his moral and mental limits. To this end, Siegel and Schuster introduced Lex Luthor in the pages of Action comics issue #26 as a megalomaniac bent on world domination. In his first appearance, Luthor had amassed an army by way of mind control and was in the midst of pitting two unnamed European countries against one another when Lois Lane stumbled upon his plan. Sending a note to Superman through a soldier who was unaffected by Lex Luthor's devices, Lois Lane was rescued and Lex Luthor was defeated. Testing the waters a second time, Luthor returned in Superman issue #4 in 1940, during which time Siegel and Schuster established Superman's moral limits in addition to his wits.

With Lex Luthor challenging Superman to a series of tests regarding his strength, speed and durability, at the conclusion of their conflict, Superman threatened to throw Luther into his own plane, cracking his skull in the process. While Luther admitted defeat, this situation illustrated the darker nature of Superman during the Golden age in that he was willing to kill and in the case where someone willingly threatened his life or the life of someone around him, expressed little remorse over their deaths.

However, as time passed Joe Schuster's eyesight began to deteriorate, but because Superman's popularity was at a fever pitch leading to appearances in World's Finest and other DC publications, Schuster was unable to keep up with the increased workload. In response he launched his own studio and hired on artists such as Jack Burnley, Fred Ray, Wayne Boring and Al Plastino, all of who would become known as some of the most iconic artists for the Superman title. During this time however, the world was changing: Germany had already invaded Poland and World War Two was underway.

With the United States remaining neutral for both political and social reasons, Superman's comics in the early days of world war two maintained his role of fighting criminals and corrupt politicians, as well as saving the day; but after the Japanese attack on Pearl Harbor in 1941 leading to a declaration of war by the United States, Superman, like nearly all comic book superheroes reflected this, in that his stories saw a shift from fighting on American Soil to fighting overseas. While the Superman Comics never actually used names like Adolf Hitler and Benito Mussolini, the propaganda within his stories was clear: Superman supports the Allied troops and so should you.

By 1945 at the close of World War 2 following the surrender of Japan aboard the USS Missouri, as the most popular title DC had at the time, the Superman comics began to shift their focus back to the United States. With Dick Grayson introduced as Robin in 1940 with Detective Comics number #38 and serving as a driving force in the popularity of Batman among children, DC looked to incorporate this element into the Superman Mythos as a way to expand on his character and increase sales. To this end, in January of 1945 under the writing and artistry of Siegel and Schuster, DC officially launched Superboy. Appearing for the first time in More Fun Comics Issue #101, because of Superman's popularity, Superboy was an immediate hit among fans. Introducing concepts like Superman's hometown of Smallville, Superboy provided fans with the evolution of Superman by filling in the gap between in his arrival on earth and his adoption of the Superman Mantle. This combined with Superman Issue #53 in 1948 retelling his origin story as well as introducing Jor-El as Superman's father meant that during a time when the popularity of Superheroes was on the decline following the end of World War 2, Superboy and Superman were actually gaining popularity.

During this same year, and after its creation in the Superman radio show in 1943, under Byron Woolfolk, fans were met with the comic book introduction of Kryptonite. Originally depicted as red in color, Kryptonite's first introduction in the comic books explains it had arrived on earth following Krypton's destruction and served to provide a weakness to Superman in that it stripped him of his powers, placing him on an even playing field with weaker villains. Serving as an aspect of his character that made him all the more relatable which in turn fueled the flames of his popularity, in the eyes of fans, it seemed as though the publications of Superman were nothing short of perfect, a sentiment that would continue on during the Silver age under the watchful eye of Mort Weisinger, largely considered to by the one of the revolutionary editors of the Superman title.

CHAPTER

3

Expansions
and
Copyright

By 1952 the success of Superman and Superboy was undeniable. The Man of Steel had captured the imagination of millions and his comics sat on shelves around the world. Conversely Superboy had provided fans with the life of Clark Kent following his arrival on earth leading up to his dawning of the Superman mantle. However, the issue faced by DC at the time came with the popularity of superheroes was rapidly fading in the post-world war 2 era, to be replaced by science fiction comics and invaders from outer space.

> **...the popularity of superheroes was rapidly fading in the post-World War 2 era, to be replaced by science fiction comics and invaders from outer space.**

Where Science Fiction itself dates back to humanity's attempts to explain what they didn't understand, throughout the ages, science fiction and humanity held a shared evolution, in that as society grew more adept and technologically advanced so too did science fiction, allowing for more complex and intricately told stories feeding on the conscious and subconscious mind of its reader, permitting for tales of fantasy or transportation to realms of terror. While Thomas More's Utopia, Jonathan Swift's Gulliver's Travels and Mary Shelly's Frankenstein stand as some of the most well-known stories from the 1500's, 1700's and 1800's respectively, with Pulp magazines having remained steadily popular in the 1920's and 1930's, the Golden age of Science Fiction found its roots in the 1937 publication Astounding Stories.

Created by Hugo Gernsback, largely considered to be one of the most influential science fiction writers of all time, Astounding Stories came out of previously published works within the pages of Modern Electrics and its successor, Electrical Experimenter, both of which focused heavily on the technical nature of electricity and electrical components for the novice hobbyist. Where these Magazines did see short science fiction stories as back up features, following the success of early Pulp magazines, Hugo Gernsback released Astounding Stories as the first Science Fiction publication of its kind, functioning as an anthology series containing science fiction stories. Renaming the publication to Astounding Science Fiction the following year, the stories within contained early writings from the then 19-year-old Isaac Asimov, as well as Arthur C. Clark and Robert Heinlen. Resting in the shadow of Superman, Batman, Captain America and others but slowly gaining steam, because the popularity of superheroes was rooted in the patriotic propaganda of World War 2, at the conflict's conclusion, the emotionally and physically exhausted American Society looked to other means of entertainment as a way to shift their focus from real world conflict to imaginary suspense. With Science Fiction providing an escape by way of suspending disbelief and looking to the stars, the Golden age of Science Fiction saw the same explosive rise as comic books, giving way to radio shows like 1938's War of the World's, an anthology radio drama famous for causing a mass panic with johnnycome-lately listeners believing an alien invasion was actually occurring.

> **...the golden age of science fiction saw the same explosive rise as comic books...**

Intending to keep up with the changing times and revitalize interest in superheroes, under the direction of DC editor Julie Schwartz, and later Gardner Fox best known for creating characters like the Green Lantern Alan Scott, the Flash Jay Garrick, and the Justice League predecessor the Justice Society of America, DC effectively rebooted its continuity for the very first time bringing an end to Golden age and initiating the start of the Silver age, paying special attention to not only Superman, but Batman as well.

...DC effectively rebooted its continuity for the very first time bringing an end to golden age and initiating the start of the silver age...

Created in 1939 by Bill Finger and Bob Kane as a billionaire by day and vigilante by night, while Superman did stand as the first Superhero, Batman's popularity arose by way of incredible wealth and extraordinary physical training which in turn, represented the peak of human ingenuity. As DC's top two characters at the time, the first comic depiction of the two being featured together came with New York World's Fair issue #2. Originally designed as a comic counterpart to the 1939 World's Fair in Flushing Meadows New York, issues 1 and 2 were intended to provide a depiction of various fictional characters' experiences at the fair or centered on the nature of the fair itself. However, because the event was designed as a one off and issue #2 sold out completely, in 1941 the New York World's Fair comic was rebranded to World's Finest, renumbered to issue #1 and contained a series of solo stories involving Superman and Batman alongside Dick Grayson.

While this remained the standard for the next 12 years, in 1952 with Superman issue #76, the two officially met for the very first time. Spearheaded by Edmond Hamilton, a writer for some of Superman and Batman's best stories in the late Golden and early Silver ages, the story saw the duo attempt to stop a criminal escaping with stolen diamonds, revealing their identities to one another, and serving to confirm that the superheroes of DC comics existed in a shared universe, opening the door for a long term friendship between Batman and Superman as well as laying the foundations for the introduction of the Justice League in 1956.

At the same time, with Superman's own solo title and Action Comics coming under the control of Editor Mort Weisinger, as he stated in an interview with Guy H Lillian III titled The Man Who Wouldn't Be Superman, during a conversation with a friend after taking over the title, Weisinger was told that the super hero genre was essentially a passing fad with the characters contained within being unable to last any real measure of time. Taking it as a challenge and sinking himself into the publications, from Weisinger's perspective, there seemed to be no real explanation as to why Superman possessed the powers of flight, X-Ray Vision and super strength. Instead, readers were simply expected to believe that this came as a byproduct of his physiology and the effects of Earth's gravity. However, because the realm of Science Fiction contained as much fact as it did fantasy, Weisinger looked to the explosively popular introduction of Barry Allen in 1956 whose powers originated in an experiment gone wrong, reasoning that these concepts of fact and fiction could be intermingled into the superhero genre, providing an explanation of Superman's fantastic abilities. Conversely, while the stories of Superman had their roots in the man of steel fighting criminals and corrupt politicians, with the exception of his supporting cast, there was very little name recognition in his comics which instead focused on run of the mill villains of the week. Intending to correct these problems and others in an effort to create a more cohesive and tight knit continuity, Weisinger was also forced to contend with the fact that fans guarded their hero with jealous eyes and were avidly against anyone making changes that deviated too far from the original content.

...these concepts of fact and fiction could be intermingled into the superhero genre, providing an explanation of Superman's fantastic abilities.

Looking to find a balance by placating older fans and drawing in new fans, where the early stories stated that Superman's powers were tied directly to his physiology in addition to Krypton's gravity in relation to earth with Superman issue #53 introducing Jor El as the father of Superman, under Weisinger's direction and as part of DC's overarching soft reboot, the intended changes were rolled over into the mythos, introducing Kryptons Red sun as a reason for not only why Kryptonians didn't have powers on their own planet, but more so than that provide the basis behind superman's new abilities.

As it was explained, the gravity of Krypton is several times more intense than earth and so when Superman arrived the difference in gravity allow for both super strength and flight. In addition to this, the ultraviolet rays emitted by Earth's yellow sun hardened Superman skin, making it impenetrable to earth's weapons as well as enhancing his five senses allowing him to achieve extraordinary feats. Furthermore, the stories of Superman began to include real world celebrities with the man of steel appearing on This Is Your Life with Ralph Edwards, Candid Camera with Allen Faunt and even went as far as to make references to the physical similarities between television personality Steve Allen and Clark Kent.

Continuing to expand on Superman and his place within DC, in 1954 and 1958 at the direction of Weisinger, writer Otto Binder created two stories titled Superman's Pal Jimmy Olsen and Superman's Girlfriend Lois Lane in order to focus on the Man of Steel's supporting Cast without sidetracking from his main stories, but also introduced the bottled city of Kandor. Referencing Weisinger's Interview with Guy Lillian, when the idea was initially pitched to DC's executives, Weisinger was met with hostility under the notion that neither Jimmy Olsen nor Lois Lane were popular enough to hold their own series. However, Weisinger himself had actually reached out to his target demographic, speaking with children directly on why they enjoyed the stories of Superman and whether or not interest was there for a bolstering of his titles. Coming to the conclusion that fans were clamoring for most anything that expanded on Superman's publications, following the launch of The Adventures of Superman in 1952 starring George Reeves, because actor

Jack Larson had brought Jimmy Olsen to life in such a way, the Jimmy Olsen spinoff series was released to critical success, allowing DC to launch Superman's Girlfriend Lois Lane, which went on to become the third most popular title behind Superman and Superboy. Regarding Kandor, with Action Comics issue #242 seeing the debut of Brainiac as one of Superman's most longstanding villains, instead of introducing the villain as a run of the mill character, instead, Brainiac was established as having hailed from an unnamed planet, visiting Krypton in the past and shrinking the city of Kandor, placing it in a bottle. Where Brainiac existed largely as a plot device throughout Superman's silver age stories, the concept of Kandor served to bolster Superman's own culture in that with the city being unable to return to its normal size, Superman seemed so close yet so far away from being able to restore some variation of his home planet.

CHAPTER
4

Rough
Times

Not all was pleasant for the Man of Steel's comics however. In 1947, while still remaining employed as content creators, Jerry Siegel and Joe Shuster had hired their friend and attorney Albert Zugsmith, filing a lawsuit against the newly merged Detective Comics and National Allied Publications on the grounds that the original 1938 contract failed to take into account Siegel and Shuster's desire to see Superman in varying forms of media outside of comics and that the contract lacked mutuality under the idea that Superman was an unrealized concept and was still in the process of being developed when it was sold arguing that the depiction of Superman in the late 1940's was a wholly different creation from their original work. However, presiding Judge J. Addison Young had found in favor of National Allied regarding Superman, stating that Siegel and Shuster were given first right of refusal and that the contract was for work previously performed.

On the matter of Superboy however, because the publication had been introduced by Siegel and published by DC, the character was not a derivative of Superman and instead, was a wholly separate entity. Where the legal battle saw Siegel and Shuster settling out of court by selling the rights to Superboy for 200,000 dollars, as fallout of the situation, both Siegel and Shuster were terminated from DC Comics, their names were dropped from all future Superman and Superboy related comics leaving the two uncredited with the heroes' creation for almost 40 years.

> ...both Siegel and Shuster were terminated from DC Comics, their names were dropped from all future Superman and Superboy related comics leaving the two uncredited with the heroes' creation for almost 40 years.

That said, while Siegel and Shuster were forced to walk away empty handed, with the Silver age basis for Superman established and well received by fans, once again under the expansive direction of Mort Weisinger, writer Jerry Coleman introduced the fortress of solitude in 1958 with Action Comics issue #241. Initially appearing without an explanation of how it was built, the Fortress of Solitude was designed by Superman is a place of solace, accessible only through the use of a giant key and functioning as a way to keep safe elements of his Kryptonian heritage, but also as a tribute to the most important individuals in his life with rooms dedicated to various villains including Lex Luthor and Metallo, but also friends like Lois Lane, Jimmy Olsen and Batman.

Furthermore, because the reception of Superboy indicated that the public was open to new versions of Superman, DC looked to expand on the Man of Steel's role in their lineup, as well as reach out to the demographic of women and young girls by creating a female counterpart that would serve in a support role to fight alongside both Superman and Superboy. Created in 1958 by

Otto Binder, Supergirl's introduction came by way of Jimmy Olsen discovering a totem that granted three wishes, one of which was used to create a female sidekick to help Superman out, but also emphasized a compelling story centering on Lois Lane. As the main love interest of Superman, Otto Binder sought to build speculation on the possibility that Lois Lane was being replaced in an effort to drive controversy among fans and in turn spur interest in Supergirl's introduction. As a source for both Superman and Supergirl fighting together, the comic was also relatively short in that Superman had discovered a bridge washed out, he was able to repair it in time to avoid a train pile up and discovered that the entire scenario was a trap set by unknown criminals looking to kill Superman by exposing him to green Kryptonite. With Supergirl intervening to save Superman, her demise came about when she picked up green kryptonite knowing the danger it represented, but after removing it from Superman's immediate vicinity while exposing herself to its radiation for too long, she succumbed to its fatal effects. Making her way back to Jimmy Olsen, she asked him to wish her out of existence something he agrees to do.

Following the story, fan reaction to the concept of Supergirl was overwhelmingly positive with thousands of letters pouring into the head offices of DC Comics. As a result, Kara Zor El, the most well-known version of Supergirl made her appearance in the pages of Action Comics issue number 252 in 1959 and was created once again by Otto Binder. Providing a true backstory for the Character this time, Otto Binder established that Kara Zor El's family survived the explosion of Krypton alongside several others. Hailing from Argo City which remain unnamed until Action Comics #316 in 1964, Supergirl's origin story established that following Krypton's explosion, the chunk of rock they were living on became an irradiated chunk of Kryptonite. Placing a layer of lead on the ground to keep themselves protected, a meteor shower took place, shredding the protective material and polluting the atmosphere with the effects of Green Kryptonite.

> **...fan reaction to the concept of Supergirl was overwhelmingly positive with thousands of letters pouring into the head offices of DC Comics.**

Seeing no option besides sending their daughter away in an effort to save her life, Kara navigated the cosmos, eventually locating the Earth after realizing that Superman had been sent that planet and had been endowed with superpowers after his arrival. To this end, Kara's parents chose Earth as the safest location, and using a rocket ship similar to the ship of Superman, after which she encountered the Man of Steel, was enrolled in an orphanage and adopted the mantel of Supergirl. Remaining hidden from the world for 10 years until Action Comics issue #285 after which she was publicly revealed by Superman, with their newest creation in hand, Super Girl was rolled over into her own series under Adventure Comics and alongside Superboy and Krypto the Superdog, opened the door for a host of new characters to be introduced into the Superman family including Comet the Super Horse, Streaky the Supercat and Bepo the Super Monkey.

At the same time, within the greater DC Comics itself, questions remained involving the characters of Flash and the Green Lantern. With the Silver age seeing the removal of Jay Garrick and Alan Scott who in turn were replaced with Barry Allen and Hal Jordan without an explanation, in 1961 DC launched a story called The Flash of Two Worlds which served to establish the multiverse in stating that the version of Superman and others who appear between the dawn of the DC Comics in 1938 up to the introduction of Barry Allen in 1956 existed in a separate universe called Earth-2 with the current versions existing in a reality called Earth-1. However, by 1962 fans were beginning to notice a trend: with Mort Weisinger operating as sole editor of all Superman related titles, and seeking to add something new every six months to the Superman landscape, almost all continuity prior to Weisinger's introduction as editor in 1957 was either being completely ignored or rewritten. As an example, in 1960 with Adventure Comics #271, Jerry Siegel who had since returned to writing for DC in a marginal capacity established that the hatred between Lex Luthor and Superman dated back to the Man of Steel's years as Superbly when he met Lex Luthor as a teenager.

> ...seeking to add something new every six months to the Superman landscape, almost all continuity prior to Weisinger's introduction as editor in 1957 was either being completely ignored or rewritten.

Originally a fan of Superboy and looking to become the world's greatest scientist, Luthor had developed an antidote to kryptonite, but when a fire broke out, Superboy used his super breath to put the fire out, destroying Luthor's experiment in the process. Losing his hair and blaming Superboy by claiming that he was jealous of Lex Luthor's intelligence, as the year's past and Superboy grew to become Superman, Luthor's animosity deepened and was used to explain his early appearances in the Superman comics and why he had such a hatred for the hero.

Where some of these changes angered hardcore fans due to the idea that their favorite stories from the time between the Silver and Golden ages were being ignored, in the end it served the purpose of creating a more tight-knit continuity that allowed for existing readers to pick up the Superboy titles, read about an encounter and pick up with its fruition in the Superman titles or one of its related books. While this did benefit existing fans, it also began to create a web of nightmares for potential fans. Following the introduction of the DC multiverse in 1961 and the crossovers that came with it, prospective readers looking to get into Superman comics were met with a massive interweaving of stories that began in one comic and concluded over the course of several others. As a result, these potential fans found themselves frustrated and in doing so, began to take notice of a competitor who is introducing heroes that didn't gain their abilities from a Yellow Sun, but of the effects of Cosmic Rays and genetic mutations.

Where some of these changes angered hardcore fans due to the idea that their favorite stories from the time between the Silver and golden ages were being ignored, in the end it served the purpose of creating a more tight-knit continuity...

CHAPTER

5

Competition Builds Character

By 1962 Marvel Comics had introduced the Fantastic Four as a response to the Justice League of America. Led by the now infamous duo of Stan Lee and Jack Kirby, The Fantastic Four shot Marvel to instant success which was then capitalized on with the introductions of Spider-Man, The Incredible Hulk, Thor, Iron Man, the X-Men and the Avengers. Forced to share the limelight with their competitor, DC had to find ways to make Superman more accessible and fast or they stood to lose their position as the top company in the world of comic books. To this end, in 1962 under Edwin Hamilton, Action Comics issue #293 saw the return of Red Kryptonite.

> **Forced to share the limelight with their competitor, DC had to find ways to make Superman more accessible and fast or they stood to lose their position as the top company in the world of comic books.**

Previously introduced in Adventure Comics #252 in 1958 over the course of various comics, Red Kryptonite was established to affect Superman in random ways with no two samples working the same way. Making his return in Action Comics, Edmund Hamilton used this to launch a story called "The Feud between Clark Kent and Superman" which saw a sample of Red Kryptonite splitting the Man of Steel into two distinct personalities: The heroic Clark

Kent and the villainous is Superman. Following this trend, in 1964 with Justice League issue #29, DC introduced Earth-3 as a Universe opposite of the Earth-1 continuity which saw the first appearance of the Crime Syndicate, a group consisting entirely of evil versions of DC's characters with this version of Superman, called Ultrarman.

Try as they might, while these stories were aimed at maintaining existing readership and bringing in new readers, it only served to complicate the Superman landscape, and so by 1970 with Mort Weisinger retiring from DC after a thirty-year career, Julius Schwartz stepped up, taking over the series and all of its related publications. Under the era of Julius Schwartz however, where Weisinger had a more grandiose view of Superman, Schwartz wanted a more tamed down version that returned the Man of Steel to his Golden age roots. To achieve this goal, Superman's titles were quite literally taken to the chopping block, with E. Nelson Birdwell taking over Lois Lane Girlfriend of Superman, Mike Zekowsky taking over Adventure Comics and Murray Boltenoff taking over Action Comics, Superman's Pal Jimmy Olsen and Superboy, leaving Julius Schwartz in charge of Superman proper and World's Finest as well as miscellaneous team ups between Batman and the Man of Steel.

Believing Superman to have become too powerful and his landscape too convoluted under Weisinger, Schwartz brought in Dennis O'Neil who had been writing the Green Arrow and Wonder Woman titles, and along-side the aforementioned editors cut a swathe in the Man of Steel's continuity, eliminating Kryptonite which Schwartz believed had become an overused plot device, canceling the Imaginary Stories Line which served as a series of publications outside of the existing Superman continuity, merged Lois Lane Girlfriend of Superman and Superman's Pal Jimmy Olsen into Superman Family which served as an Anthology for the previously mentioned comics among others in addition to killing off Mr. Mxyzptlk, Bizzarro and Titano, as well as Krypto the Dog, arguably the most famous animal in DC Comics.

With 1971's Superman #233 initiating the Sandman Saga which saw superman's power reduced as well as his return to fighting villains on earth for the majority of his stories, because fans were writing in by the droves demanding a return to cosmic adventures and the threat that came with them, by the time the Sandman Saga concluded with Superman #242 in 1971, DC cancelled the new Superman rebranding and replaced Julius Schwartz with Cary Bates. However, in the eyes of fans the damage had been done and following the restoration of Superman's status quo in 1972, the Man of Steel began rapidly shrinking into oblivion.

Going back for a second, in 1939 following the critical success of Superman, the fledgling comic book industry found itself on the cusp of a new generation of entertainment media, but also in a sort of quagmire. If Superman changed the definition of heroes in terms of how they were represented in literature and his popularity had taken the world by storm, how could his popularity be matched?

If Superman changed the definition of heroes in terms of how they were represented in literature and his popularity had taken the world by storm, how could his popularity be matched?

In an effort to answer this question as well as gain a foothold in the increasing popularity of comic books, writer Bill Finger and artist Bob Kane created Batman. While Batman's early concept art depicted his physical appearance in a far different manner than what we know him to be today, one thing that didn't change was the basis behind his character. In contrast to Superman's incredible feats of strength, endurance and various powers due to his alien physiology, Batman was simply a man who was victim to a tortured past. With no real powers of his own, Batman would rely on a combination of his intelligence and wealth, and by extension various gadgets and technologies in order to fight crime within Gotham City. Furthermore, Batman's outlook on the world was a total 180 from Superman in that Batman was ruled by his inability to let go of the death of his parents, a road which governed every decision in relation to friends and partners. Superman on the other hand was the last of his kind and while both had a personal understanding of how quickly life could be lost, Superman chose not to take a darker outlook on life and instead, cherished the possibility of what people could become.

> **Batman's outlook on the world was a total 180 from Superman...**

While the introduction of Dick Grayson in 1940 saw a massive increase in sales of the Batman and Detective Comics titles, with comic books gaining a larger and larger following among America's youth in the world overall, the industry was not without its critics. Considered to be one of the most well-known, in 1954 psychiatrist Frederick Wertheim released a book titled Seduction of The Innocent which argued that the violent nature of comic books adversely affected children, predisposing them to violent acts themselves. While the book is considered to be nonsense by today's standards, at the time and with comics sweeping throughout the United States as the largest source of entertainment among America's youth, the book drew the attention of various political and parents groups, leading to the creation of the Comics Code Authority.

Formed in 1954 by the Comics Magazine Association of America which had existed to regulate the content of comic books in the face of public criticism, the comics' code was designed to replace Governmental Regulation as a set of guidelines that defined what was considered appropriate for comics themselves. While companies were not required to adhere to the code, their refusal to do so resulted in a lack of sales as distributors refused to purchase and sell comics which did not feature the code of approval on the cover. At the same time, because the code of approval contained rules which included the prohibition of demonizing Governmental entities, using words like horror or terror in the title as well as glorifying crime by allowing criminals to escape punishment, with the core of Batman's titles focusing on vigilante justice, in a lot of ways, DC's hands were tied regarding their ability to write stories which could maintain the essence of what made Batman popular while ensuring sales of comics.

...DC's hands were tied regarding their ability to write stories which could maintain the essence of what made Batman popular while ensuring sales of comics.

As a result, and because the publications of the Batman comics in the 1950's and early 1960's saw both Batman and Robin as well as their supporting characters like the Joker, the Penguin and Two-Face reduced from being overly serious and violent to being less serious and sometimes even gimmicky, fans came to view the publication as yet another victim of the comic's code.

Where DC had tried to boost interest in the series by introducing Batwoman and Batgirl in 1957 and 1961 respectively as heroes who could assist Bruce Wayne in battle, these creations combined with the introduction of Bat-Mite in 1959 by Bill Finger and Bob Kane as an imp using technology from the 5th dimension all failed to reinvigorate interest with many fans maintaining their distance from the title. To this end, with Superman's popularity at an all-time high under the control of Mort Weisinger as well as his part time involvement in the Justice League and his escapades within both the Superboy and Supergirl titles, in truth, the crossovers between Bruce and Clark within the pages of World's Finest seemed to be the only thing keeping Batman from being cancelled forever. However, while the comics' code maintained its hold on the Comicbook Industry, regulating content and allowing Superman to remain the top seller in DC comics, society itself was beginning to shift away from these standards and move in the direction of acceptability with regards to storytelling, character design and interaction.

Coming out of 1971's The Night Gwen Stacy Died as well as the Green Arrow stories and the anti-comics code campaigning of Stan Lee, this time period saw the early forming of darker stories. Prior to this era, the idea of a superhero failing so disastrously as to allow his love interest to die was unthinkable and whether by Spider-Man's own actions or the actions of the Green Goblin, the fact remains that Gwen Stacy's death moved comics away from fantasy and began focusing on more realistic depictions of heroes in terms of their humanity and their shortcomings.

During this time, Marvel Comics Editor-In-Chief Stan Lee had been approached about writing a story involving drug use within Marvel Comics. Finding itself predated by Neal Adams and Dennis O'Neil's classic Snowbirds

Don't Fly within the pages of Green Arrow Volume 2 issues 85 and 86 which focused on Oliver Queen's sidekick Speedy becoming addicted to Heroin, while O'Neil and Adams' work focused on the unglamorous side of drugs and its impact on the lives of its users, the precedent was set allowing Stan Lee to initiate his story under the guise that drugs in comics had already been approved. Using the situation as a way to campaign for the Comics Code's modification, by the end of 1971 going into the start of 1972, the Comics Code began to see a series of modifications which chipped away at its rigid standards allowing for the publication of stories dealing with drugs, political corruption and the return of horror themes.

CHAPTER
6

The Death of Superman

Where the market as a whole began to see a paradigm shift with comic books becoming darker and focusing on the grittier element of humanity, instead of allowing the Man of Steel to follow these trends, instead, Superman's comics largely remained lighthearted and adventurous. However, the issue faced with this standard of storytelling was that after a while, either the Superman landscape would become too convoluted due to the Weisinger's desire to constantly expand, or the stories would become mundane with the Man of Steel fighting the same villains over and over again.

> ...the market as a whole began to see a paradigm shift with comic books becoming darker and focusing on the grittier element of humanity...

Looking to keep this from happening, in the early 1970's following his departure from Marvel, writer and artist Jack Kirby moved to DC where he began work on his cosmic odyssey and the creation of the fourth world line. Taking over Superman's Pal Jimmy Olsen under the direction of Editor Murray Boltenoff, Jack Kirby set about introducing the villain Darkseid in the pages of issues #134, #135 and 1#36 as a background villain of enigmatic origins. While Kirby would eventually depart over creative differences before the story could be completed, his work was rolled over into the larger DC universe under the direction of Julius Schwartz who had taken over the Superman title following Weisinger's retirement.

Now where Superman would continue on through the difficulties described earlier, his escapades with Batman remained all hallmark of DC's line up keeping both heroes relevant amidst the growing climate. While Bruce Wayne himself would see a series of revitalizations of his own by way of Dennis O'Neil, Neil Adams, Dick Giordano and others, much like the introductions of Batgirl, Batwoman and Bat-Mite, these modifications failed to draw readers going into 1985's Crisis on Infinite Earths.

Now where Superman would continue on through the difficulties described earlier, his escapades with Batman remained hallmarks of DC's line up keeping both heroes relevant amidst the growing climate.

Viewing the line wide reboot as a way to provide readers with an updated depiction of the character, because Frank Miller had been setting the world on fire with his run on Daredevil, DC contacted Miller for the purpose of revitalizing interest in Batman with a more updated depiction for the modern age. Taking place within the pages of The Dark Knight Returns, the dystopian graphic novel focused on a much older Bruce Wayne returning to the superhero landscape pending the start of World War 3 and a Gotham City immersed in crime. While the brunt of the graphic novel dealt with Bruce Wayne overcoming the physical issues facing men of a certain age and attempting to eliminate the crime within Gotham, as part of his goal to revitalize Bruce Wayne, Frank Miller cast aside the decades of friendship in place of a rivalry.

With Superman becoming an agent of the Government and Batman making Gotham City the safest place in the Country, the embarrassment faced by the Federal Government who were coming to be viewed as inept in comparison to a caped vigilante, Superman was instructed to remove Bruce Wayne from his position, sending Gotham back into chaos and allowing the nation to look towards the Federal Government for their security.

> **...the conflict between Batman and Superman was as much metaphorical as it was literal...**

Culminating in a battle between the two, the conflict between Batman and Superman was as much metaphorical as it was literal in that where Superman had been experiencing a downward turn in popularity following the retirement of Weisinger, the void of DC's top hero was left open for Batman to take. Seeing the Dark Knight Returns conclude with Batman overpowering Superman using a specially enhanced mechanized suit, after informing Clark that his life is continuing strictly because Bruce allowed it, fans essentially abandoned Clark Kent by the droves, transitioning their favoritism to Bruce Wayne and his darker method of storytelling. Ushering in the start of the Bronze age and comics which focused on how the world really was as opposed to how it could be, DC experienced a mad dash in their efforts to revitalize Superman culminating in the Death of his character in 1992.

Ushering in the start of the bronze age and comics which focused on how the world really was as opposed to how it could be, DC experienced a mad dash in their efforts to revitalize Superman...

CHAPTER

7

Near Collapse

ollowing Crisis on Infinite Earth's and the reconciliation of all the alternate universes and their removal from existence with DC's most popular characters being folded into the main continuity referred to as New Earth, the Superman series was taken over by former X-Men artist John Byrne who would spend the next three years effectively re-telling Superman's stories and providing a new foundation for his character. Debuting with the six issue miniseries The Man of Steel which focused on a new origin in the Post-Crisis continuity, the miniseries served to streamline DC's flagship character, eliminating all the different forms of Superman including Supergirl, Superwoman, Superboy and the Super pets, setting the iconic hero back to his roots as The Last Son of Krypton.

At the same time, only the most important of characters remained including Lex Luthor who was transformed into the now widely recognized wealthy industrialist with sinister schemes, harkening to the familiarity of Marvel's Kingpin as he had been envisioned under the direction of Frank Miller.

After this, in September of 1986 going into the month following Man of Steel, the works of John Byrne set the stage for the future of Superman's ongoing titles. Initiating a new series of publications, the solo Superman series was renamed to Adventures of Superman under the writing of Marv Wolfman and Jerry Ordway, with John Byrne launching a new Superman solo series titled Superman Volume 2 and continuing Action Comics which remained as volume 1. Looking to maintain the themes of the post-crisis continuity in focusing on content which could be easily accessed by new fans, the life and times of Superman were arranged by John Byrne in the form of 3 four issue miniseries titled World of Krypton, World of Smallville and World of Metropolis, all of which existed to provide the reader with a strong understanding of Superman's heritage, his new life on Earth as a child, and his adulthood in Metropolis.

With many fans viewing the series' as the other half of the Superman coin, providing greater emphasis on his supporting cast and continuing the themes of his own solo series, the idea of changing this status quo seemed a bit extreme to say the least.

In addition, one of the boldest moves in DC was their attempt at reforming the entirety of the Action Comics line. With many fans viewing the series' as the other half of the Superman coin, providing greater emphasis on his supporting cast and continuing the themes of his own solo series, the idea of changing this status quo seemed a bit extreme to say the least.

On the other hand, DC's logic seemed sound in that the idea of Action Comics and Superman sharing a singular series of events was one of many problems that led into fan confusion and the launch of Crisis on Infinite Earths in the first place. To this end, where John Byrne's time under the title featured team ups between Superman alongside both well-known and lesser known heroes in DC, with issue #600, the title was renamed to Action Comics Weekly, returning to its anthology roots of the Golden age and featuring only 2 pages of Superman related content while also serving as a platform for the introductions and reintroductions of both new and previously existing titles including the Secret Six, Deadman, Wild Man and Phantom Lady.

Finding itself to be a critical success among new readers looking to access DC following their Crisis Reboot, the beauty of this anthology came in that readers now had a multitude of stories with differing styles of art work, allowing for a diverse line up and exposure to heroes who would have otherwise fallen to the wayside.

The drawback to this was that because of Schwartz's actions in the 1970's, the hardcore Superman reader base had all but abandoned the series, and while the possibility existed of their return, the continuity reboot of Crisis of Infinite Earth's left a bad taste in their mouths owing to the idea that the Superman they knew would never come back. As a result, for the next five years between 1987 and 1992, Superman continually slipped in relevance with fans preferring the darker and grittier stories of Batman. Faced with this fact, in the summer of 1991 during their annual Summit, DC brought in the writers and artists for the Superman line in order to find a way to restore his character to relevance. Winding the clock back to 1987, in addition to editing the Superman title alongside writer John Byrne, Editor Mike Carlin had begun the process of gathering his team for annual meetings referred to as the Super Summit, during which time the stories and themes of his titles would be planned out for the following year.

> **Superman continually slipped in relevance with fans preferring the darker and grittier stories of Batman.**

However, the issue that Carlin and his team faced was that while the Man of Steel had gained a following of sorts in the post Crisis continuity, in a lot of way, people viewed the themes of his stories as archaic in that the world had changed, and even if the wholesome and righteous ideologies of Superman held a place in the hearts and minds of some, most readers didn't identify themselves as a person who always did the right thing and always made the right call.

Instead people recognized the contradictory nature of humanity and the fact that our words don't always match our actions, but because

Superman's rigid stance of fighting villains was unshakeable and the core of what made him who he was; the idea of Carlin and his group was to create a story that would return him to relevance without destroying his legacy.

...even if the wholesome and righteous ideologies of Superman held a place in the hearts and minds of some, most readers didn't identify themselves as a person who always did the right thing and always made the right call.

During a 2014 interview with Andrew Steinbieser of Comicbook.com, writer Dan Jurgens had stated that the initial idea of Superman's Death as it had been designed at the Summit was to finally bring Clark Kent and Lois Lane together by having the two engage in marriage. Where John Byrnes 1987 story, Superman: The Secret Revealed provided the long awaited revelation to Lois that Clark and Superman were one and the same, the most noticeable attribute of their characters came in the fact that after all the two had been through, not only had they never been married, but Clark had never officially revealed his identity to Lois.

To this end, at the conclusion of a yearlong build up, DC intended to have Superman reveal his identity to Lois with marriage coming out of the decision. During this time however, Lois and Clark: The New Adventures of Superman was already in production, and as a byproduct of the deal worked out between DC's parent company Warner Bros. and ABC, DC comics and ABC had to work jointly to ensure that neither produced content that would disrupt the flow of the other. As a result, when DC announced their intentions to have Lois and Clark to marry, ABC had the company hold off as it was an idea attractive to them and they could actually make more money from the show than DC could make from their comics.

With a years' worth of stories being thrown out the window, DC was forced to go back to the drawing board in order to find a way to make Superman relevant again. Covered in the critically acclaimed short film The Death and Return of Superman by Comic and Film writer Max Landis as well as Superman Doomsday – Requiem & Rebirth: Superman Lives which focused on the events leading up to the iconic story, as one of the long standing members of the Superman Summit, writer Jerry Ordway had always ended the team's meetings with the statement, let's just kill him, and because the Superman writers were irritated that they couldn't go forward with the stories that they were working on, instead of just dismissing this as nonsense, the idea stuck. Following this, the focus of the creative teams was split into four ideals. The first was to craft a story that provided an unshakeable finality, the second was to create a villain that could actually kill Superman, the third was to provide the story of how it happened and the fourth was to answer the most important question, how do they bring him back?

...Jerry Ordway had always ended the team's meetings with the statement, let's just kill him, and because the Superman writers were irritated that they couldn't go forward with the stories that they were working on, instead of just dismissing this as nonsense, the idea stuck.

CHAPTER

8

Rebirth

Looking to the first, because Superman had been in existence for almost 60 years at the time, virtually every story that could be written had already been done. Superman had already exhausted his experiences with Lois Lane, he had battled Darkseid, and on several occasions, time travelled in an effort to prevent his planet's destruction. As a result, because of comics like 1961's issue #149 by Jerry Siegal and Kurt Swan which had already killed Superman on one occasion, the creative team was in a boy who cried wolf situation as fans had already heard this story before. In order for them to ensure that the story would sell, the creative team would need to write the events in a way that would lead people to believe that not only was Superman gone, but there existed no indication that he was ever coming back.

> **...the biggest problem regarding the Death of Superman wasn't how the story would be written, but who would kill him.**

To the second task, writer Dan Jurgens' the biggest problem regarding the Death of Superman wasn't how the story would be written, but who would kill him. Since most of Superman's most challenging villains were largely modeled after Lex Luthor and would test Superman physically rather than mentally, the only villain capable of going toe to toe against the Man of Steel at that time without external aid would have been Darkseid. However, Jurgens wanted to introduce a new villain that could kill Clark off without having to fill lingering plot holes, and if Darkseid had killed Superman and lived, the question would have to be asked what happens next regarding his character and potential conquest of Earth.

On the other hand, if Darkseid had died while fighting Superman, fans would want to know how the realm of Darkseid would change following the power vacuum. Looking to bypass this problem, Jurgens created Doomsday as a character that could eliminate the possibility of lingering plotlines by killing off Superman and dying in the process. However, simply creating Doomsday and putting him in the story couldn't be done overnight and an event of this magnitude needed a sort of buildup in order to achieve the affect that DC was looking for. The reasoning behind this was that despite his lack of sales, Superman signified the greatness of humanity and that as the father of the modern superhero, was literally the foundation upon which all other heroes had been built on.

To this end, Doomsday needed to function as the anti-thesis to Superman in that he could be devoid of emotion and concern for the wellbeing of others and represent a fundamental force of nature that couldn't be reasoned with, presenting a scenario whereby Superman had finally encountered a being of which he couldn't overcome. As a result, over the course of the month prior to The Death of Superman's release, within the pages of Man of Steel issue #17, Superman #73, Adventures of Superman #496 and Action Comics #683, DC had writer Louise Simonson among others continue the trend of Clark fighting his various foes, but at the end of each comic, a green clothed arm with bones protruding could be seen punching its way through a metal box culminating in Man of Steel Issue #18, with the first on panel appearance of Doomsday.

For the third task, following this series of lead ups, going into the main story itself, the creative team decided to use Dan Jurgens idea of a 22-page slugfest in the final issue with Superman and Doomsday fighting to the death leading into the fourth task, which was to describe the heroes left behind, the new heroes who would emerge to try to fill the void by Superman's departure ultimately culminating in his return to the comic book landscape. In an interview with Superman Through The Ages, an independently operated website dedicated to providing a chronology of Superman's history, writer Jerry Ordway had stated that in life, Superman was always taken for granted as being a selfless hero, guaranteeing the safety of Lois Lane, Jimmy Olsen, his parents and Metropolis, but that in death, mourners came out of the woodwork and overnight everyone loved and missed him. This was expanded on by Dan Jurgens stating that they had wanted to include world reaction to the Death of Superman, and provide both realistic and fictional ideals, focusing on not just friends and family, but superheroes and super villains, all of whom respected and even looked to the Man of Steel as an icon and influence.

Where some were skeptical as to public reaction of Superman's death, the move paid off, igniting a media firestorm in November of 1992 with all major media outlets including the New York Times, CNN, the Washington Post and Fox News providing their own segments on the history of Superman, allowing the title to become a critical and commercial success, selling out almost immediately with DC issuing a veritable ocean of reprints. Referencing the documentary titled as Superman Doomsday – Requiem & Rebirth: Superman Lives, with the intention of DC to kill Superman reaching the world's ears in the months prior to its release, the now iconic Superman issue #75 saw an estimated total of 3 million copies sold, making it the third highest selling comic behind X-Force issue #1 and X-Men volume 2 issue #1.

Where some argued that the story was a publicity stunt, designed to draw attention to a failing iconic hero by way of killing him as opposed to crafting sound and compelling stories, writer Roger Stern disputed these claims stating "...quite the contrary, these stories and the attention they received–all just sort of snowballed. The Publicity came later...the word got out on a slow news day, and the media sort that followed as greater than anything we could have hoped for. But it was all thanks to the story's power." However, where the Death of Superman was able to successfully drive the sales of his character's title and return the Man of Steel back to the main stage even if only for a short time, the comic and its multitude of variant covers had a side effect that would shake the very foundation of the comic book industry.

> **...the comic and its multitude of variant covers had a side effect that would shake the very foundation of the comic book industry.**

Winding the clock back to the silver age of comics in the 1950's, during this time period, the idea of comic book collecting was largely isolated to a small portion of society who actively traded their own comics at local meeting places in exchange for other stories that would complete collections or contained some measure of sentimental value. However, in the early 1960's, former coin turned comic collector Robert M. Overstreet had looked to comics with the intention of creating a pricing guide in an effort to both ensure collectors weren't being swindled, as well as provide a definitive source of income. Partnering with

Jerry Bails who viewed comics as a source of Academic Study as opposed to a literary medium, Bails' extensive notes combined with Robert's experience in collecting saw the 1970 release of the Overstreet Price Guide. Initially selling with a cover price of 5 dollars and containing 218 pages' worth of price listings, the guide also contained a definitive number of existing prints for any particular issue, serving as the basis behind determining the price for the value of a comic in relation to its accessibility. Becoming an invaluable tool of both collectors and dealers, by 1976, the Overstreet Price Guide became the standard for Comic Collecting, finding itself being syndicated on a national level.

At the same time and going into the 1980's, Diamond Distributors and Capital City, two of the largest distribution companies began to aggressively over expand, quickly nationalizing and eliminating regional competitors. As a result, these distributors and others like them became far less selective in determining how they conducted their business meaning that with as little as 300 dollars, a client could set up an account with them allowing many casual collectors to transform themselves into comic book dealers. To this end, between the mid 1970's going into the 1990's, comic book shops experienced exponential growth in that where 1979 saw as few as 800 shops, by 1993 over 10,000 existed. As a result, orders from these smaller suppliers saw an increase in comic publishing and based on the laws of supply and demand, also saw an increase in price meaning that companies like Marvel and DC went from publishing 40 titles a month in 1985 at 60 cents per issue, to 140 comic books a month for $1.25 and higher.

Wrapping back around to Superman, in the face of this revelation and after the events of Funeral For a Friend, following a 3 month hiatus, the Superman related titles were relaunched with DC announcing Reign of The Supermen as a story arc to both cash in on the continued press of Superman's death as well as explore the different variations of Superman within the greater DC Universe and orchestrate a whole sale character reboot. During this event, four new variations of Superman appeared including John Henry Irons wearing a suite of steel with the Superman crest while wielding a giant hammer, The Man of Tomorrow also known as Cyborg Superman, the Metropolis Kid Kon-El who never claimed to be Superman and the Eradicator, also known as the Last Son of Krypton. With each character having their origin and role explored in the pages of Action Comics, Adventures of Superman, Superman Volume 2 and the Man of Steel, where the reception to these characters was largely mixed, on the whole, the goal of DC was to use their presence to not only provide a depiction of what the world would have looked like without a Superman to protect it, but to also build up to Superman's grand return in the Man of Steel issue #25.

> **...the goal of DC was to use their presence to not only provide a depiction of what the world would have looked like without a Superman to protect it, but to also build up to Superman's grand return...**

Coming out of the revelation that Cyborg Superman was a villain, Man of Steel #25 established that the real Superman had been placed in a Kryptonian regeneration matrix and following the restoration of his powers and re-emergence from stasis, the newly returned Superman dawning an all-black costume with shoulder length hair led a campaign against Cyborg, ending his machinations, restoring his position as the world's top hero and officially engaging in marriage to Lois Lane.

While the Return of Superman line of stories sold well owing to the idea that it completed a concept which fans considered to have been left hanging, on the whole, the stories of Superman and his related publications never recovered in that his reader base felt betrayed due to believing that they had participated in one of the most iconic stories ever told. However, with Superman returning to life in the turn of a page and the perception of his death having been written out in such a way, the collapse of both Superman and the comic industry was all but guaranteed.

...with Superman returning to life in the turn of a page and the perception of his death having been written out in such a way, the collapse of both Superman and the comic industry was all but guaranteed.

Viewing the story as yet another example of diluted content, this alongside the realization that anyone could die and return on a whim couple with higher comic prices began to drive away the customer base and by 1995 when factoring the issue that many comic book shops were underfunded and poorly run, the entire industry had turned into a veritable melting pot of bankruptcy's with over 90%

of comic book stores closing their doors. This coupled with stories like Batman Knight Fall and X-Men volume 2 issue #1 selling a litany of copies with variant covers under the false belief that the industry was booming sent the world of comics into a tailspin. During this time as with any near economic collapse, where Marvel and DC were holding on for dear life, smaller publishers like Valiant Comics were going under or being sold to other companies while collectors themselves saw their comics becoming almost entirely worthless.

While some publications like Action Comics #1, Detective Comics #27 and Amazing Fantasy #15 would retain most of their value owing to their introductions of Superman, Batman and Spider-Man respectively, on the whole, the value of most all other comic books began to flounder without the possibility of regaining their previous value and the industry itself saw a decrease of 46 Million Comics per year to 7 Million. However, not all was lost for Superman in that while comics themselves were at an all-time low, where Superman would continue to play second fiddle to Batman, his character received a measure of reinvigoration that didn't come from comics and instead, hailed from the world of animation.

CHAPTER

9

Everything Changes

n the 3 years following the Death of Superman going into 1996, the comic book landscape had changed irrevocably. While the comic bust was still running strong and the effects were still being felt, fans were also coming to the realization that Superman was gradually taking a backseat to Batman. Led by Paul Dini and Bruce Timm's Animated Series featuring the voice talent of Kevin Conroy as the Caped Crusader, Batman had quite literally soared to the front and center of DC's line up, stepping right over the shoulders of Superman and into the limelight. With actor Mark Hamill lending his voice as the Joker and Harley Quinn stealing the spotlight as one of fans favorite characters, the fate of Superman seemed to live up to the 1986 Alan Moore story titled: Whatever happened to the Man of Tomorrow?

While the comic bust was still running strong and the effects were still being felt, fans were also coming to the realization that Superman was gradually taking a backseat to Batman.

Looking to return the iconic hero to his status as the top character, DC also recognized that the road to this goal was stiff and virtually impossible in the face of fan reception of Superman's return. The reason for this was that as the first hero, despite his twists and turns, occasionally questionable stories and adventures into space, Superman was the definitive hero. While I can offer a series of my own thoughts on this matter, I'd actually like to turn to Brian Truitt of USA Today in a 2013 article titled 'Why Superman is the greatest American Hero'. As it states:

Searching for identity is a very human concept, for sure. But what makes Superman and his alter ego Clark Kent the ultimate American hero is that he has reflected our culture and society, ever since his first appearance in DC Comics' Action Comics No. 1, cover-dated June 1938. And his crash-landing in a cornfield as a baby and being raised by two Kansas farmers is, in a way, the story of the American immigrant. Not surprisingly, it was hatched by a pair of men from Cleveland, Joe Schuster and Jerry Siegel, whose parents themselves were immigrants from Europe looking for a new start in North America. Since they created the Man of Steel in the 1930s, "the core narrative in Superman has been and continues to be the values and belief about the U.S. experience being strong enough and good enough to address the troubles facing the generation engaged with the character," says Julian Chambliss, a history professor at Rollins College in Winter Park, Fla., who specializes in superheroes and the American experience. During the Great Depression, Tarzan and Flash Gordon were popular in comics because they transported Americans elsewhere, says Brad Meltzer, a novelist and host of History Channel's Decoded. When World War II encroached on our shores, though, "America starts getting scared and here comes this giant, almost straight-from-the-flag character who's come to save us."

"The Big Blue Boy Scout" marched with the troops and fought Nazis in the late 1930's and into the '40s, but he was also "a reaction to industrialization, to the power of big business," says comic-book writer Mark Waid. "He was created as a social agitator, a character who fought for the oppressed and the weak." In the 1950s, Superman went from anti-authority to a sort of "uber-cop," since the postwar era is "where we saw ourselves as the world's peacekeepers," says Waid. And then the Man of Steel of the '60s and '70s had stories that touched on the counterculture and "young people not really having a good sense of who they were or where they came from or where they were going."

When Christopher Reeve flew onto the big screen in 1978's Superman, he had to save the world and Lois Lane, of course, but Waid also found that he exuded a relaxed attitude. "He didn't have to be histrionic, he didn't have to be war-mongery, he didn't have to be antagonistic — because he's Superman for God's sake. What threatens him?

We're in a post-Watergate, post-Vietnam era, in that brief period in American history where we felt confident and almost complacent in our place in the world." The 1980s featured Superman fighting his own hubris and self-importance, Meltzer says. The Man of Steel who appeared in Frank Miller's seminal Batman comic-book series The Dark Knight Returns in 1986 was "a perfect reflection of Reagan politics and being a heel to the government." And the '90s pit Superman against not only a bad mullet but also big corporations — his arch-enemy Lex Luthor is even redefined as a cunning millionaire businessman.

That said, with DC having killed off the iconic hero in the Death of Superman, both hardcore and casual fans as well as the general public and the press had all believed that they were partaking in something spectacular; a comic book event unlike any other which unfolded in a way that could never be repeated. However, with the Man of Steel returning, not only had this illusion been shattered, but as American screenwriter, director, producer, and actor Max Landis pointed out in his short film The Death and Return of Superman, where the industry had long since held the belief that dead heroes stay dead, they could now return without consequence, diminishing their own stories and the value of any one character in any particular situation.

Faced with this fact, DC looked to the success of Batman The Animated Series as a means to jump start Superman's return to popularity. Coming under the control of Bruce Timm, Alan Burnett and Paul Dini, the depiction of Superman within the animated series was an amalgamation of his best concepts including the Pre-Crisis portrayal of Krypton and its destruction, the character and relationship of Superman in the Silver age of the 1950's and 1960's, as well as the contemporary and down to earth nature of his abilities during the Post-Crisis era of John Byrne.

Considered to be one of the best adaptations of Superman in the modern age, during a discussion with several of my fans through periscope, a smart phone app allowing its user to livestream directly to both Twitter and fellow users, the general consensus among them seemed to be that without having ever read one of his comics, Superman the Animated Series lived up to everything they thought Superman should be: an icon for DC's superhero landscape who walked with a silent confidence while emanating an air of incredible power. Receiving a series of awards including Outstanding Sound Editing, Musical Direction and Composition as well as Best Individual Achievement, where the sales of Superman's comics continued to fall albeit at a slower rate, even if only in the realm of animation, the Man of Steel was beginning to see a slight resurgence.

...Superman the Animated Series lived up to everything they thought Superman should be: an icon for DC's superhero landscape who walked with a silent confidence while emanating an air of incredible power.

Looking to the popularity of the animated series as a way to drive interest in potential new fans, under writer Dan Jurgens, the Man of Steel was revamped into the Man of Energy, stripping him of his traditional powers in place of energy, taking a more modern approach to the original 1963 story contained within Superman issue #163. Running between February and June of 1998, this change to Superman saw very little reception owing in part to the idea that fans of the series were looking for a depiction of the character they had grown attached to through the animated series, as well as long time readers viewing the concept as a continual step away from what made Superman great.

...the Man of Steel spent the next several years in a state of flux, experiencing occasional resurgence in sales but continually remaining behind Batman in popularity.

Changing his character back to his more recognizable form with Justice League of America issue #20 in 1998, the Man of Steel spent the next several years in a state of flux, experiencing occasional resurgence in sales but continually remaining behind Batman in popularity. Considering the post–Death line of publications to have transformed Superman's comics into a veritable melting pot of confusion, in 2003 following the start of Smallville Season 3 which focused on Superman's time encountering various villains and growing into the iconic hero, writer Mark Waid looked to clear out the unnecessary content of his comics and offer a definite story of Superman, providing both new and existing fans with a starting off point for his character. Covered within the pages of Superman: Birthright, Mark Waid updated Superman for the modern times, delving into the destruction of Krypton, his arrival on Earth and eventual undertaking of the mantle, all while borrowing elements from his Pre-Crisis continuity and Post-Crisis origin as it had been written by John Byrne.

Receiving multiple awards including the American Library Association's Best Books for Young Adults, while the events contained within are thrown out of continuity during the events of Infinite Crisis which recreated the multiverse following its destruction during Crisis on Infinite Earths, for many fans, the story of Birthright remains one of the standout events from his publication history. However, as DC continued to find a solid ground for their flagship character and ensure that he remained a pivotal figure within their landscape, the issue of Siegel and Shuster pursuing the legal campaign for the rights to Superman remained in the background.

Winding the clock back to 1969, with both Siegel and Shuster having maintained a low profile in the comic landscape and DC removing their names from the Superman titles following their original 1948 lawsuit, the larger comic community remain entirely unaware of their contributions to Superman's creation, only having this knowledge provided to them by those who lived through the legal issues and in turn, passed that information on. However, when the 60th Congress of the United States passed the copyright act of 1909 adding amendments to the 1790 Copyright Act, a clause was implemented that required copyright holder to reapply for Federal Copyright protection after 28 years. Looking to use this stance as a way to take possession of Superman through applying as the original copyright holders, the 1947 ruling of Judge Addison Young was upheld, confirming that Siegel and Shuster had given up the entirety of their rights to Superman after signing the original contract with DC.

Appealing to the United States Court of Appeals for the Second Circuit in 1974, the ruling of the lower court that Superman was a work for hire concept was overturned with the Court of Appeals ruling that where Action Comics issue #1 had presented Superman as he was designed by Siegel and Shuster, the various expansions to his character saw the basis behind his continued success, all of which was done by Siegel and Shuster themselves. While this did provide a glimmer of hope for both Siegel and Shuster, the Court of Appeals ultimately ruled against them, finding that their basis behind the creation of Superman and his introduction to DC held no bearing over the fact that they had legally signed their rights away. Turning to the court of public opinion, the knowledge of Siegel and Shuster having been the creators of Superman became common knowledge following a public relations campaign led by Jerry Siegel alongside artist Neal Adams who had long since been looking to unionize comic creators. Paving the way for the Creator's Bill of Rights as it was published in 1988, the work of Siegel, Adams and artist Jerry Robinson led to DC parent company Warner Brothers offering a lifetime stipend of 20,000 dollars a year to both Siegel and Shuster as well as reinstating their names as the creators of Superman and Superboy in addition to having made contributions to various other aspects of the Superman landscape.

Fast forwarding to 1996, with both Siegel and Shuster having passed away and their widows taking possession of their estates, the campaign of the Siegel and Shuster family to regain the rights to their creations had actually taken two separate roads. Where the sister and nephew of Joe Shuster had signed a contract in 1992 relinquishing their rights and agreeing to stop pursuing future rights to Superman in exchange for a 25,000 dollar a year stipend, the Siegel estate looked to the Copyright Act of 1976.

Covered in Brad Ricci's book Super Boys: The Amazing Adventures of Jerry Siegel and Joe Shuster – the Creators of Superman, with the Copyright Act of 1976 establishing that the original creators of copyrighted content could terminate their partnership with an existing copyrights holder and regain their rights after a term of 56 years, the law as it was written during this time presented the Siegel estate with its best chance of retaking both Superman and Superboy. Filing a notice of termination with Warner Brothers, in October of 1996, DC countered by offering the heirs of Jerry Siegel a payment of 3 million dollars, an annual stipend of 500,000 dollars, a 6% royalty of Superman, a 1% royalty of his publications, and full medical benefits.

Expecting to move forward with both Estates settled, in November of 2001 the Shuster estate hired attorney and Pacific Picture producer Marc Toberoff who argued that because the original wording of the 1976 Copyright Act stated that only the wife, children and grandchildren of a creator were able to legally sign away the rights of the Shuster estate, the 1992 contract between the Shuster estate and DC held no bearing and was effectively null. In addition to this, with the Siegel estate still in the midst of negotiations with DC, all dicussions were halted, the Siegel family fired their original attorney and hired on Marc Toberoff owing to the idea that the Sonny Bono Copyright Term Extension Act of 1998 allowed for a larger window to terminate a partnership between the content creator and the copyright holder. Looking to help the Siegel and Shusters win their copyright case and purchase the rights to Superman for his own production studio, attorney Marc Toberoff filed a notice of termination on behalf of both the Siegel and Shuster estates for the Superman and Superboy concepts.

Spanning the course of 12 years between 2004 and 2016, the legal battle between the Siegel and Shuster estates for the rights to both Superman and Superboy was well documented in various forms of media who followed the news story as one of the most pivitol example of the complex nature of US Copyright Law. Appearing before Judge Stephen G. Larson on October 30, 2006, in his March 2008 public opinion statement following the case's conclusion, where DC argued that the 2001 contract between the Siegel estate and DC constituted a binding agreement that prevented and future pursuits of copyright, Judge Larson argued that neither DC nor the Siegel's actually came to an agreement owing to the constantly changing terms of the contract leading to a halt of negotiations and the Siegel's hiring Marc Tarpoff. Granting the Siegel's their rights to Action Comics #1, with Superboy having been created as a derivative of Superman, the rights for his character were removed from DC entirely and returned to the Siegel estate. Appealing to the United States Court of Appeals for the Ninth Circuit, the ruling of Judge Larson was overturned and handed back down to the circuit courts in 2013 with Judge Otis Wright upholding the agreement between the Siegel estate and DC citing California Civil Code sections 1619 through 1633 which provide for verbal contracts to be legally binding under the assumption that the contract will be signed at a later date. As a result, the rights of Superman, Superboy and all related titles were removed from the Siegel estate and returned to DC.

...the rights of Superman, Superboy and all related titles were removed from the Siegel estate and returned to DC.

Conversely, where Marc Tarpoff and the Shuster estate maintained their half of the rights to Superman, in 2010, DC sued the Shuster estate arguing that because Joe Shuster himself had willed his estate to his sister who in turn signed their rights away in 1992, future considerations for the right to terminate were invalid. Siding with DC, the Shuster estate's half of the rights to Superman were returned to DC.

That said, where the legal battle between DC and the estates of Siegel and Shuster saw Superman and Superboy fluctuating in the pages of their own comics in the mid 2000's, with DC rebooting their lineup in 2011 with the New 52, Superman experienced a revamp of both his costume and mannerisms. Establishing that the superheroes of the world had only appeared in the last 5 years, the stories of Action Comics and Superman's publications served to provide two sides to the same coin in that Action Comics took place 5 years in the past with Superman undertaking the man of steel mantle and his solo series focusing on the modern day. Where existing fans of Superman expressed disdain at the change of his costume, the larger controversy arose from his view of the world. With the Pre-New 52 Superman representing the vast legacy of DC and appearing as a kind of father figure for the Superhero universe, his New 52 version was more akin to a late 20's early 30's man trying to find his place in the world. On the other hand, fans and society as a whole had grown accustomed to the more experienced and wiser Superman, and while this change did provide a change of pace and a plethora of new stories, ultimately, the title continued to slump, consistently resting around the bottom of the top 50 comic releases for each month, leading to the return of the Pre-New 52 Superman at the start of DC Rebirth as a means to reinvigorate interest in his sales.

The History

Since the 1930's, Superman has been the poster-child for what a hero is. He's a treasured icon, a symbol and so much more. His stories have him saving the earth, fighting for his political beliefs and always standing on the side of justice. But this decorated path has come with its share of turmoil. From controversial story-arcs to failed films, the Man of Steel has not always been as perfect as his powers would make you think. This is Superman, in a Snapshot, faster than a speeding bullet! More powerful than a locomotive!

1930'S

- Siegel and Shuster start a new project by creating a crime fighter who is above the law.

- He's what we call an anti-hero.

- Terrorizing criminals but ignoring laws.

- His powers around the time of Hindenburg included his legendary speed and strength, as well as, his less prominent ability today of jumping stretches of miles in a beat.

1938

- This all came to fruition in 1938. #ActionComics

- This origin story has him as a reporter by day, hero by night.

- The son of Krypton, his linage as an alien raised on earth is still to this day one of his most identifiable characteristics.

1940'S

- Other KEY element of Superman, his bald nemesis: Lex Luthor.

- Introduced in the 40's, Lex is a genius who exploits anyone he can for his own satisfaction.

- It is around this time that Superman's ability to fly is first introduced.

- He has become virtually indestructible and can even time travel!

- More powers, captivating villains and a heart of gold, Superman quickly rises as the definitive comic of choice for every American child.

- The Adventures of Superman, a radio series starring Bud Collter is launched as a result of this Superman craze.

1941

- 8 shorts are created as a result of the booming popularity. Superman, now a cartoon, reaches more children than any other character to date.

1945

- Given the interest by children across the nation, Superboy is created.

1950'S

- In the early 50's, The First TV series named "The Adventures of Superman" aired starring George Reeves.

1958

- The alien Braniac enters the scene. From the planet Colu, his advanced technology makes for a spectacular balance to Sperman's brute strength.

- Continuing on the line of creative challenges for Superman, Bizarro.

- A grey-skinned version of Superman, Bizarro is what would have happened if Superman had gone bad.

1959

- By the end of the 50's Supergirl joins the team to help Kent and Superboy combat a collection of villains.

1960'S

- The 60's brought along a sense of logic and intrigue for our hero.

- The association of the sun's rays to his powers is developed as well as the narrative of his history with Lex.

- In Superman #146, published on July 1961, his powers are defined as being solar-dependent with his muscular powers, super strength, speed, and flight, attributed to gravity and the sun.

1970'S

- In the early 70's, the comic version of Superman had a career change.

- The onetime newspaper reporter was promoted to a television news reporter.

- Joining him on set was Lana Lang, causing a tension with Lois Lane.

1973

- In the world of TV, the "Super Friends" were created.

- The "Super Friends" consisted of a 30 minute cartoon where other DC heroes would join Superman on adventures.

1978

- Richard Donner casted Christopher Reeve as Kal-El in the late 70's.

- These films built in Clark's origin, his powers and his nemesis: Lex Luthor.

1980'S

- Superman II hit the big screen after the success of the original.

1983

- By 1983 Superman III was in theaters.

- This movie dealt with the mind of the Man of Steel.

- From questioning his powers to exploring his role in society, Superman III was a new look for the character.

1985

- Crisis on Infinite Earths, 12 issues published by DC resulted in the death of Superman and a reimagining of the character by writer Alan Moore.

1987

- Theatrically, Superman IV was under production with a release date of 1987.

1990'S

1992

- Superman Dies. DC Comics kills Superman! The hero suffers major injuries in a fight with Doomsday which results in him dying in Lois Lane's arms.

1993

- Dean Cain dawns the cape in the early 90's in Lois & Clark, The New Adventures of Superman.

1996

- Crisis on Infinite Earths, 12 issues published by DC resulted in the death of Superman and a reimagining of the character by writer Alan Moore.

2000'S

2001

- Live action on the small screen was Clark's next adventure.

- Smallville, a TV series based around Kent's like prior to becoming Superman began airing in 2001.

2003

- Smallville establishes that the "S" shield Superman is famous for has a double-meaning of both Super and Hope.

2006

- In 2006, a sequel of the Reeve movies are attempted in Superman Returns.

- With the sequel failing to capture the hero Reeve portrayed, the series was rebooted.

2013

- Man of Steel premiered with Henry Cavill as the lead.

- As a result of Man of Steel, Warner Bros. green-lit a movie that sparked the interest of the entire world: Batman v Superman.

In the coming years we will see the Justice League in the big screen, we will see more redrafts and new angles in comics and TV. But when it is all said and done, the Man of Steel, Kal-El, the Son of Krypton, Clark Kent will always be the great hero. The first hero. Superman.

Afterword
BEHIND THE CAPE

"Now a staple of the superhero mythology is, there's the superhero and there's the alter ego. Batman is actually Bruce Wayne, Spider-Man is actually Peter Parker. When that character wakes up in the morning, he's Peter Parker. He has to put on a costume to become Spider-Man. And it is in that characteristic Superman stands alone. Superman didn't become Superman. Superman was born Superman. When Superman wakes up in the morning, he's Superman. His alter ego is Clark Kent. His outfit with the big red "S", that's the blanket he was wrapped in as a baby when the Kent's found him. Those are his clothes. What Kent wears – the glasses, the business suit – that's the costume. That's the costume Superman wears to blend in with us."

Bill, Snake Charmer. Kill Bill: Vol. 2

So as someone who has been reading comics for the better part of 20 years, it was always an accepted idea that Superman was the original. Standing alongside Batman and Spider-Man as the holy trinity of recognizable comic book characters, in truth, Superman remains the franchise of not just DC Comics, but the comic book industry as a whole. I remember getting into comics by way of X-Men the Animated Series, the 1992 show based on a combination of the X-Men team and the X-Factor stories, and while my desire for more knowledge was largely rooted in the Marvel Universe, in the back of my mind, Superman always stood there.

A few months ago, I was scouring the web searching for some inspiration for a logo on a personal project when I came across a list of the most recognizable symbols in the world. While most of these symbols come as the writer's own personal opinion, the comments of these differing blogs offer some measure of scrutiny regarding the list itself and the author's view. Where the blog contained symbols belonging to name brands like Nike, BMW and McDonald's, the iconic triangle around an S stood as the author's opinion as the most recognizable symbol in the world. While this does bring validity into the question, especially in comparison to the various religious symbols of the world, it does highlight the silver lining: Superman isn't just a comic book icon. He's a human icon.

My passion for Superman is rooted in the very notion that iconic heroes and their comics aren't about mindless fights with bad guys or pulling multiple planets out of a dying galaxy, they're about imagination and suspension of disbelief melding with our desire for something greater. Assuming that you've read the entirety of my book or at least the chapter focusing on the rise of Batman, you'll know that Superman's own publication sales have dropped in the face of the Caped Crusader pummeling the mentally ill during the night. What's funny about this though is that while Batman's movies have proved to be more complex and have resonated stronger with audiences, the Man of Tomorrow remains one of the most iconic symbols in the world.

Assuming that DC recognizes this and I can't see how they wouldn't, the return of the classic Superman during the events of DC Rebirth hold the strong possibility of his character returning the age of beautiful storytelling and personal struggles. While only time will tell, even if things don't pan out the way we hope, at the very least, we can look to the days of old and take solace in the fact that a time existed when the Man of Tomorrow stood as the most popular fictional character in the history of literature.

ACKNOWLEDGEMENT

When I first started my YouTube channel, I had been working as a dispatcher for my local university. Focusing on facilities management, my job at the time had 3 core tenants: life safety, human/creature comfort, and energy conservation. I imagine that if my former supervisor and coworkers are readings this right now, they're probably laughing at that last little bit.

Throughout my time on the job, I found that the position wasn't very fulfilling and I looked to the realm of YouTube as an outlet. For years I had been told that I would make an excellent teacher and combining this with my love for history and comics, the decision became clear: make videos on the history of comics. Looking around the geek culture sphere at the time, because most channels were dedicated to explanations on components of characters like their powers or their gadgets, there didn't seem to be much in the way of explanations on why those characters were made and how they changed over the years. Setting my sights to task, my first video came in the form of

Jason Wyndgard, a mutant and enemy of the X-Men who operated under the moniker of Mastermind due to his ability to manipulate and control the 5 senses. Posting my work to the Marvel Comics subreddit at reddit.com, I moved on to a handful of other discussions including the philosophy of Galactus' role in the Marvel Universe and how the multiverse worked, but it wasn't until the announcement of Scarlet Witch and Quicksilver in Avengers 2 that everything took off.

As one of Marvel's most well-known characters following the House of M whereby she altered the very fabric of reality itself, my explanation of Scarlet Witch drew in viewers who looked to know more about her character in response to the upcoming film. This combined with the 3-month long project of explaining 2006's Civil War event led to my channel growing at a geometric rate. Finding myself partnered with other fledgling YouTubers who I now count as friends, we formed the The Weekly Pull brand and I gave my supervisor a month and a half notice, vacating my position at the beginning of 2014. Taking up YouTube full-time, my journey into the realm of new media led to appearances at a multitude of comic book conventions and encounters with fans.

To be honest, while I and the rest of The Weekly Pull had ran into subscribers occasionally during our convention appearances, our first meet up took place in San Antonio Texas as part of our trip to Six Flags. Announcing the date, time and location on Twitter, we found ourselves surrounded by around 25 people, all of whom had come across our content at some point or another and looked to meet us. During this time, Marvel had recently launched their Secret Wars event and released a series of new stories containing variant covers, one of which was completely blank save for the title. Purchasing this comic and having each fan sign it, this bit of literature stands as one of the most prized possessions I have, resting on a book shelf in a display stand for all to see.

So whether you're someone who has seen every video I've ever made, met me at a convention or have no clue who I am and picked up this book out of sheer curiosity, this is dedicated to you.

AUTHOR BIO

Robert Jefferson is a Lexington, Kentucky based YouTuber specializing in comic book related content with over 20 years of involvement with comic books. He attended the University of Kentucky for 2 years but departed after finding success on YouTube by way of creating videos designed to explain comic book characters, teams and concepts in an easy to understand way. Robert Jefferson's work on YouTube had subsequently led him to form a joint effort with several other comic book YouTuber under the banner of The Weekly Pull in addition to speaking publicly at various venues including the Rhode Island Comic Book Convention and Penny Arcade Expo.

CPSIA information can be obtained
at www.ICGtesting.com
Printed in the USA
BVOW07s0554300716
457366BV00003B/5/P